D1613610

Table of Contents

Rourke
Educational Media
rourkeeducationalmedia.com

Can you find these words?

court

kneepads

point

setter

Let's Play!

I play volleyball.

I am on a team!

I wear a uniform.
I wear **kneepads**.

kneepads

We play on a **court** with a net.

court

Don't let the ball hit the court!

setter

The **setter** bumps the ball into the air.

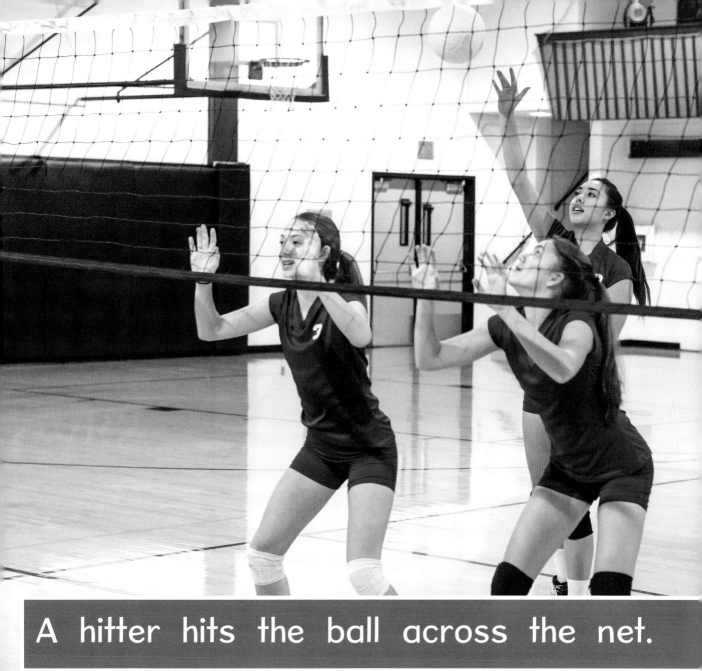

A hitter hits the ball across the net.

It hits the court on the other team's side.

We score a **point**!

point

Sometimes we win.
Sometimes we lose.

We always have fun!

Did you find these words?

We play on a **court** with a net.

I wear **kneepads**.

We score a **point**!

The **setter** bumps the ball into the air.

Photo Glossary

 **court** (kort): An area where sports such as basketball are played.

 **kneepads** (neepads): Special equipment athletes wear to protect their knees.

 **point** (point): A unit for scoring in a game.

 **setter** (SET-tuhr): The player in charge of the offense, deciding who gets the ball and setting up the hitters.

Index

About the Author

Elliot Riley is the author of dozens of books for kids. When she's not reading or writing, you can find her walking by the water in sunny Tampa, Florida.

www.rourkeeducationalmedia.com

PHOTO CREDITS: Cover: ©Matt_Brown; p2,3,5,7,8,9,14,15: ©FatCamera; p2,10,14,15: ©miodrag ignjatovic; p12,13: ©monkeybusinessimages

Edited by: Keli Sipperley
Cover by: Rhea Magaro-Wallace
Interior design by: Kathy Walsh

Library of Congress PCN Data
Volleyball / Elliot Riley
(Ready for Sports)
ISBN 978-1-64369-118-3 (hard cover)(alk. paper)
ISBN 978-1-64369-119-0 (soft cover)
ISBN 978-1-64369-217-3 (e-Book)
Library of Congress Control Number: 2018955842

Printed in the United States of America, North Mankato, Minnesota

3 1327 00668 9699